1-20-23

LIMERICKS FOR POST-ELECTION SANITY

"A Patient Man Named Joe Watched Trump Refuse to Go..."

Odes to the
Messiest, Wackiest, & Wildest
Presidential Transition in Modern History

Written by Gregg Robins
Illustrated by Charity Russell
Edited by Karen Olson-Robins

ISBN 978-2-940693-01-6

Illustrated by Charity Russell
Edited by Karen Olson-Robins

From the same author and illustrator:
"Silenzio, Sound the Alarm!"

To "K"

This book is for my darling wife "K"
For enduring my rhymes every day
For her editing flair
All her love, and her care
I'm much more grateful than I can say.

Table of Contents

Preface
Searching for Sanity

Following the tense US elections of November 3rd, 2020, I spent a full week in my living room glued to the television, watching CNN virtually round the clock. There I monitored the fate of my country of birth and of citizenship, as if from my own personal war room, an iPhone in one hand and an iPad in the other. And then a breakthrough occurred: on November 7th, Joe Biden was finally projected the winner and president-elect by CNN and other news outlets.

I welcomed the news with tired yet joyful tears, as I sat alone staring alternately into my three screens. It was a bright new and long overdue day for America, or at least so I thought.

In concert with the projection being made, Donald Trump and his supporters ramped up their already massive disinformation campaign. This subsequently picked up steam and appeared to be a nascent effort to overthrow, or at least to delegitimize, the new president-elect. It felt like a gut punch, and I wanted to speak out, to lash out, to express my unequivocal condemnation of the insanity of what appeared to be a blatant attempt to overturn the results of the election and to violate the rule of law. I turned to social media, but rather than writing prose, or songs, as I have done in the past, I penned a limerick, what I called an 'ode to Joe.' As a singer-songwriter, I was no stranger to rhyming in verse, though I had never before tried my hand at limericks. It felt good, cathartic, and right. (Warning — if you are now considering writing limericks, they are great fun and highly addictive.) Writing my first limerick that day marked the place this book truly began. They say an apple a day keeps the doctor away. Well, I continued writing my odes every day and sharing them to keep the frustration away - or at least to lessen it.

Friends encouraged me, and I began to feel that, in some small way, I had a voice to add amidst all the rancor and strife. In the pages that follow, I offer these limericks, which represent my impressions of prominent people, institutions and events, as well as important trends that have played a role in the political morass of the past few months. My goal is to capture the absurdity of, and to find the humor in, what has transpired, even as the situation is fraught with danger and continues to evolve as I write.

The title of the book is the beginning of a limerick intended to capture the essence of the transition:

A patient man named Joe
Watched Trump refuse to go
He kept his cool
And ignored the fool
So desperate to steal the show.

While Trump's brazen attempts to delegitimize Biden's victory may have been a sideshow in the strictest sense of the word, the gravity of the numerous efforts to undermine President-elect Biden and his growing team ultimately led to the frightful, dangerous storming of the Capitol. Further, the assault on the Capitol occurred in the midst of a COVID-19 catastrophe that has devastated the country and cost countless American lives, all on the watch of and, to a large degree, the fault of the Trump administration.

Amid so much tension, drama, and uncertainty, laughter is certainly an important escape and source of comfort. My wife and I are both grateful for the laughs from late-night comics, to whom a few of these limericks are dedicated. Comedy works best when it parodies reality, and there has been a bonanza of people, institutions and events ripe for mockery in recent times. I also strongly believe that each joke contains a kernel of truth, especially the better ones. Over the centuries, court jesters have spoken truth to power to declaim the ills in their societies: dressed and seen as fools, they were often castigated for their musings.   Nevertheless, their voices were important, and while I have no intention of sporting a costume, I hope that some truth will ring out from my humor as well. The limericks that follow, while meant to be entertaining, are also intended to call out egregious behavior, and do not hide the biases of the author, particularly where strong condemnation is warranted. And while these limericks are not intended to be chronicles or historical records, they do track many events in a linear way through the transition process, which is thankfully and mercifully coming to an end as I write these lines.

This book is divided into a few collections of limericks, covering the opposing sides in the political struggles and battles in the US. It begins with "Donald Trump & His Enthusiastic Enablers" followed by "Joe Biden & His Determined Restorers." From there, the focus shifts to the institutional and international perspectives of the ongoing conflicts, with "Dramatic Days & Diminished Institutions" and "Emboldened Autocrats & Embattled Allies." Finally, the book concludes with an Epilogue, in which I offer a few thoughts on the events we have witnessed, with my optimism intact despite everything. I attempt to single out the people who have risen above the fray to strive to help the country and our world move to a better place as we begin 2021, and to whom we all owe our admiration as well as a significant debt of gratitude.

In terms of style, while limericks generally do not have titles, mine do. This is because they were each written as 'odes' to someone or something.

This book would not have come together without the encouragement, input, and enthusiasm of many others, to whom I am very grateful. The book is dedicated to my wife, who inspires me in many ways — provoking creative thoughts and then promptly editing them to make them even better. A number of people, in particular, have offered me motivation and encouragement along this short, bumpy journey. I am grateful to my Bronx brethren: Steve Kraft in Zurich, for so often making me smile with twists on my twists; Adam Insler in New York, for pushing back on some of my partisan musings, for which I still offer no apology, and Dr. Robert Silverman, also in New York, who would object if there was not an ode waiting for him when he awoke each day. Dona Schwab, as ever, was always supportive and encouraging, as were Charles Adams, Vlad Berezansky, Stuard Detmer, Stephanie Olson, Paul Polman, and Wilfried Vanhonacker. Eric Stevenson, from his Paris perch, always brought enthusiasm, smiles and support.

Since my own decision to share my limericks with friends, there have been many among them who have commented consistently, which was always very motivating and heartening, helping me to understand that I was creating something that people valued rather than just pontificating in my post-election vortex.

A big thanks to all of them for their encouragement and support.

My sincere gratitude goes as well to illustrator Charity Russell, for bringing her talent, creativity and imagination to bear on this project. As an author, it is a thrill each time to see her drawings bring ideas to life. Charity's professionalism and delightful demeanor only make the process that much more of a pleasure.

Finally, and importantly, while laughter is good for all of us, I have decided that beyond simply entertaining people, I would like to help others in the process. As a result, the proceeds from this book will be donated to a worthy cause that helps to promote much-needed social welfare in the midst of this terrible pandemic.

And with that, I leave the limericks to speak for themselves. May you enjoy reading them as much as I have enjoyed creating them and sharing them with you.

Limericks for Post-Election Sanity

1.

Donald Trump & His Enthusiastic Enablers

Justice

There once was a man from Trump Tower

Who, defeated, became awfully sour

And flail as he may

There would soon come a day

When he and his flock would lose power.

Dashed False Hopes

On election night Trump seemed to boom

As his numbers continued to zoom

When the red mirage faltered

His lead quickly altered

Thus commenced the slow path to his doom.

Fealty

This circle of women and men

Were so proud to be Republican

They would aid and abet

Hoping soon we'd forget

Something history will not in the end.

"Truth"

Oh, the president lied and he lied
Which, for him, was a great source of pride
It was all quite astounding
And the lies kept compounding
As he'd just begun hitting his stride.

Loyalty

This man by the name of Mike Pence
So seldom appeared to make sense
Shielding Trump like no other
And married to "mother"
The truth is the guy is just dense!

Decline

A clownish old lawyer named Rudy
Showed willful neglect of his duty
Once "America's mayor"
Now Trump's lead soothsayer
It's a tale of a fail, and a beauty.

Cowards

There was no greater coward than Mitch
Who could obfuscate without a hitch
The truth was right there
But with lies everywhere
He'd pretend not to know which was which.

The Fall of Pompeo

There was once a Secretary of State
Who would tarry, not accepting his fate
Though he lied and he lied
Said he'd not step aside
The world, undeterred, would not wait.

Hide & Seek

A prolific President Trump

Stayed tweeting to escape his slump

Suggesting he hurry

Aides started to worry

As mobs waited for him to stump.

Peas in a Pod

Ivanka and Jared got hired
And believed they would never be fired
They both thought they were royal
Despite all, remained loyal
But said voters: "Your time has expired."

Youngests

It's a sad tale of youngest son Eric
Who became every day more hysteric
No vote fraud could he find
Though he wracked his weak mind
Did he know the results are numeric?

Eldests

When not valiantly hunting large game
Don reaps profits from his family name
As he fans his ambitions
Lashing out at physicians
It's all in 'The Art of the Blame'.

Bursting Bubbles

Bannon pushed for "America First"
Betting Trump would deliver the worst
He guided the ship
Till it started to slip
And as happens with bubbles, it burst!

Hoaxes

Trump incessantly cries "It's a hoax!"
And he's good at convincing some folks
"Russia's acts were not real!"
"The election's a steal!"
Would be funny if these were just jokes.

Canaries

Michael Cohen decided to flip
And not to go down with the ship
As he sang to the press
And still more to Congress
He sure seemed to enjoy the whole trip.

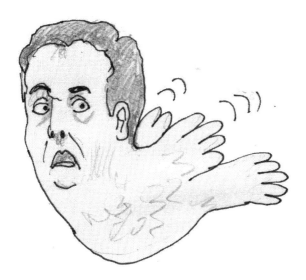

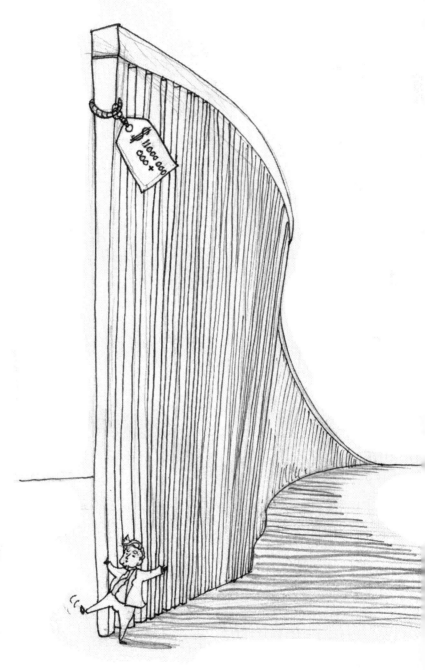

Costly Games

The long-promised wall never came
As the list grew of people to blame
Though Trump still insisted
Mexico just resisted
It was all little more than a game.

Reversals

What has happened to Stephen Miller?
For whom each immigrant was a killer
As his policies raged
Many children were caged
Now he's gone — it's the end of this thriller.

"Ethics"

There once was a man named Bill Barr
Who took his malfeasance too far
He swerves and he slimes
Unconcerned by the crimes
Just to make his boss feel like a czar.

Sliding Down

It is said about Governor Christie
That his eyes grew increasingly misty
When receiving the news
Trump was going to lose
His path down then seemed frightfully twisty.

Reveries

Ben Carson will soon have his freedom
Though in no way did we ever need 'im
No results would he reap
He was mostly asleep!
While he dreamed of the day that they'd free 'im.

Spinelessness

There once was a man named John Bolton
Who found his old boss quite revoltin'
He did not testify
And thus helped hide the lie
Which he certainly knew was verboten.

Reality

While tweeting of fraud in his residence
As he searches in vain for some evidence
The world moves along
And Trump plays the same song
Not the stuff we expect from our presidents.

Lemmings

A lackey named Senator Graham
Sheltered Trump every day and caused mayhem
Shifting truths into lies
That mad gleam in his eyes
He'd do anything not to betray 'im.

Regret

There once was a gloomy First Lady
Who knew that her husband was shady
She'd grin and she'd bear
And sometimes she'd swear
While hoping he'd never hit eighty.

Downward Spirals

Unable to change the elections
Or to stem the slow drip of defections
Trump stayed hidden away
Yet again, not his day
Next stop - the Department of Corrections.

Thanksgiving Turkeys

Trump pardoned the turkey they'd send
Mike Flynn - his old, trusted friend
There'll be more we abhor
As he goes out the door
But in January, this will all end.

Landscaping Possibilities

The "Four Seasons" was chosen to host
The press briefing Trump flaunted the most
It was just a landscaping
With the difference quite gaping
And the crowd thought they'd just seen as ghost.

Delusion

Trump remains firm in his mind
That his loss remains his to unwind
Shopping court after court
Like some ludicrous sport
Unaware that our justice is blind.

Too Little Too Late

We've now seen a torn William Barr
Who realized he'd gone way too far
He raced to recover
And soon would discover
It's too late to hide who we are.

Foresight

We don't often see Kelly Anne
Who saw the wreck coming and ran
She'd a family to save
Which, while certainly brave
Set her free from the mess she began.

Collusion

Roger Stone, with his fear of the law
Simply wanted the court to withdraw
Said Trump, "Find some techniques
To avoid Wikileaks
And deny everything that you saw!"

Blind Ego

Trump demands the vaccines bear his name

While ignoring the hurt and the pain

One more glaring delusion

Leaving zero confusion

'bout a man who just cannot feel shame.

Great Expectations

Laying claim to amazing success
"Warp Speed"'s rollout produced quite a mess
Then in White House updates
Blame was placed on the states
Whose votes they'd tried hard to suppress.

Not Working

Being president should be a job
Not a platform to cheat, lie, and rob
COVID does not retreat
Yet all he does is tweet
Every day to send grist to the mob.

Incompetence

Scott Atlas has swiftly departed

And won't finish the damage he started

He railed against masks

As he failed at most tasks

"Farewell Scott," we say most wholehearted.

Missing Par on COVID Relief

In the end, Trump decided to sign

Millions suffered, but he was just fine

Again golfing all day

His resistance would fray

At some point along the back nine.

Insiders Trading

In Georgia, one Senator Perdue

Traded stocks on the secrets he knew

Did so without a care

Bought and sold everywhere

Only pausing for lies he would spew.

Just Deserts

The people of Georgia had spoken

Record numbers of them were awoken

Democrats had prevailed

Both Republicans failed

And resumed trading stocks most heartbroken.

Debunked Strategy

The new year brought run-off elections

As all Georgians made their selections

Still Trump's claims persisted

His supporters resisted

Then lost through their own dumb defections.

Minority Mitch, Part 1

For days Mitch was going through hell
And did not take his demotion well
Feeling slightly deflated
And still aggravated
He slowly slipped into his shell.

Minority Mitch, Part 11

Minority Mitch took the floor
This hoax he could stomach no more
"Biden comfortably won
This has stopped being fun
And I recall the oath I once swore."

Christmas Zen, Part 1

The White House has its own Mister Grinch

Who thinks stealing elections a cinch

Each day pardons galore

They say "yes," he says "more!"

While Biden does not even flinch.

Christmas Zen, Part 11

"Mister Grinch" ignores all the advice

He has lists of who's naughty, who's nice

His trusted friend Twitter

Makes him think he's no quitter

Though deep down he most surely thinks twice.

Changing Tides

It seems that Bill Barr's on the outs
He seldom appears as he pouts
He performed his key role
As Don Trump's loyal troll
While neatly concealing his doubts.

Prime-Time Pandering

Thirteen Senators simply don't care
For they know of no fraud anywhere
Watch them kick, scream and pose
To see who gets a rose
On the pilot of "Who'll Be Trump's Heir."

Senator Sleaze

Rules don't appeal to Ted Cruz
Who will do anything not to lose
Plead fake cases to Court
Shaft voters for sport
While extolling the system he screws.

Great Awakenings

Breaking news: Mitch McConnell awoke
No more silence, he finally spoke
Declared Biden the winner
Complimented the sinner
Then commended the system he broke.

Delusional Seclusion

Trump unleashed a mad mob on DC
Then he watched it at home on TV
He tweeted, "They cheated"
Not feeling defeated
With so many more crooks yet to free.

Belated Epiphanies

The bold resignations are flowing
And Trump's cronies' departures are growing
But it's surely too late
To rewrite their fate
Or to replant the seeds they've been sowing.

Impotence

For Twitter enough is enough
After four years they're sick of Trump's stuff
Now without his addiction
And his spread of warped fiction
He has no way to say it's a bluff.

Miscalculation

Josh Hawley saw his chance to rise
Lift his brand on a pile of lies
But his plan self-destructed
With the Capitol abducted
As supporters were dropping like flies.

IMPEACHMENT, THE SEQUEL
(OFFICIAL TRAILER)

COMING SOONISH

20 FEBRUARY 9TH 21

Donald Trump & His Enthusiastic Enablers

The sequel will soon be released

Trump's back — they cannot tame the beast

This time he's got a mob

And he's out of a job

If you liked "Call Ukraine," it's a feast!

Directed by
The Senate

Produced by
The Taxpayers

Inevitability

Trump's cabinet continues to shrink
On a ship getting ready to sink
As the mutinous crew
Watch the captain just stew
They're desperate to wash off the stink!

"Winning"

As Trump's four years quickly wind down
He seems more and more of a clown
His acts more erratic
Congress more Democratic
And soon he himself will leave town.

One-Way Streets

There was no veep more loyal than Pence
He was not one to sit on the fence
But his skills for survival
Could not squelch the arrival
Of Trump's most ungrateful two-cents.

Payback

The Dems were surprised by old Mitch
Who thought he would make a quick switch
He said, "Trump has to go
Why, he's just a RINO
He'll soon see, without me, life's a b*tch!"

Strange Bedfellows

Nervous joy, Democrats could not hide
As McConnell had endorsed their side
At the end of their rope
They'd all push out the dope
While astonished their fates were allied.

Floating Away

Since the coup, there passed nearly a week
Before Trump felt emboldened to speak
Once again he denied
Everything he'd decried
With no paddle, he heads up sh*t's creek.

Making History

Trump's the first to have been impeached twice
Raised the bar up a notch with his vice
If he had some more time
He'd concoct a new crime
Which would help him to make it to thrice.

"So Much Winning"

Trump said we'd get tired of winning

So often our heads would be spinning

As his shameful term ends

He has lost all his friends

And his troubles are only beginning.

Toddlers

A child is well-formed by three
Thanks to Trump that is now plain to see
Throwing fit after fit
While his friends quickly split
Now still three, he's a retiree.

Limericks for Post-Election Sanity

11.
Joe Biden & His Determined Restorers

Confidence

There once was a man from Delaware

Who'd been hearing Trump whine, but didn't care

He followed his course

Without any remorse

As he knew, one day soon, Trump would not be there.

Progress

As Trump and his minions depart

The transition now nears a true start

So our country, today

Can start paving the way

For a new team and new course to chart.

Diversity

In Biden's new administration

There's a team that now looks like the nation

All colors and creeds

To meet many needs

Which warrants a standing ovation!

Guarantees

When questioned on inauguration
Joe spoke without pause to the nation
"I most strongly agree
To take Trump's guarantee
That he'll already be on vacation."

The Future

We'll soon have a VP named Harris
On the same day when we'll rejoin Paris
Make the Muslim ban go
Rejoin WHO
And that day we will cease to embarrass.

The President-elect

With the election all said and done
There's no doubt — it's Joe Biden who won
So we won't grant a pass
On the question of class
Biden takes all, and Trump still has none.

Creative Solutions

Trump's team thwarted the president-elect
Who would highlight the snubs he'd detect
As his frustration grew
Not quite sure what to do
He urged the sad bunch to defect.

Youthful Impatience

With urgency on the environment

John Kerry will meet the requirement

Quick to speak was young Greta

Who said, "Hey! John you betta

Reverse it before your retirement!"

Diplomacy

The world hears "America's back!"
There's a fresh team to get things on track
With new man Tony Blinken
There'll be lots of rethinkin'
As "America First" fades to black.

Sudden Promotions

One day Chuck learned he would be leader

No longer credentialed cheerleader

He savored the role

With his heart and his soul

As he longed for more skill as a Tweeter.

A New Conductor

Soon arriving for duty: Ron Klain

To help de-link "West Wing" from "insane"

He's beyond qualified

Will have truth on his side

And, in his case, a truly good brain!

Competence

Treasury will be run by a she
For the first time in our history
And the story worth tellin'
Is the talent of Yellen
Which will bolster our economy.

Talent

Joe historically chose Mayor Pete
As he knew Pete could think on his feet
One more seat at the table
For a man clearly able
To sort out the chaff from the wheat.

Madame Speaker

The House has a Speaker named Nancy

Who steers votes that don't meet her fancy

As she holds her positions

And enforces conditions

She knows how to make Trump feel antsy.

Gravitas

Obama certainly did his part

With attacks that were all very smart

His book sales now soar

As the crowds they do roar

He's made taking down Trump quite an art!

Change-Agents

Working tirelessly for a decade

Stacey Abrams ensured progress be made

She grew new voter rolls

Boosted turnout at polls

So that Georgians would have an upgrade.

Overcoming Challenges

Facing crises of epic proportions

As the White House engaged in extortions

Governors did their best

Tried to rise to the test

Despite POTUS's mental contortions.

Soft Power

Whatever you may think of Sanders
You cannot suggest that he panders
Since Joe Biden's big day
He's not been in the way
And he's one of the best reprimanders.

Perspective

When election news first reached Tim Kaine

"¡Muy bien!" cried he, showing some strain

"It's been such endless drama

I have so missed Obama

And I've yet to get over Ukraine!"

Suspended Disbelief

Ambassador Michael McFaul

Felt alarm when he heard of Trump's call

"He cannot press Ukraine

For his own selfish gain

It's the White House, not 'Better Call Saul'!"

Cool & Informed

The Pod Save guys helped us to cope
With the whims of a dominant dope
Their cool insider views
Helped make sense of the news
Bringing new ideas mixed with old hope.

Raging Bob

We've a debt to the great Bob DeNiro
Who for years said that Trump was a zero
Getting under Trump's hair
With his toughness and flair
The star actor has become a hero.

Redemption

'Twas just a few short years ago
That Garland heard Mitch tell him "No!"
"You will not have your hearing
An election is nearing"
And now Mitch is not cast in the show.

Wise Men

Would that we had heeded Bill Gates
Who warned we'd be in dire straits
He said, "You need a plan
Headed by the right man
Not the chaos that this one creates."

Courage

We all owe a great deal to dear Mitt

Who held firm each time Trump threw a fit

The lone GOP vote

For impeachment, of note

Who knew the tweets came from a twit.

Limericks for Post-Election Sanity

III.
Dramatic Days & Diminished Institutions

Wrongdoing

Elections should lead to concessions

In boom times as well as recessions

But never before

Even in times of war

Have we seen in their place such transgressions.

Hubris

Seventeen states have now joined the coup

An election result to undo

They charge to the Supreme

With a full head of steam

But no case that would merit review.

Higher Thinking

The Court says we're all fit to choose

Where to worship, though much we could lose

Though if God had a say

On where people could pray

Surely safety would headline the news.

Rejection

In the highest court in the land
Trump chose to make his final stand
Backed by scores of his cronies
One big bunch of phonies
He lost, as did his failing brand.

Not for Sale

More than sixty odd cases thrown out
As our judges remove any doubt
They're our crucial defense
'gainst Don Trump and Mike Pence
And thank goodness they would not sell out.

Karma

All the courts uniformly said "No!"
With time fast coming for him to go
So he tried to coerce
As this loss was his curse
And he saw we do reap what we sow.

Bipartisan Hypocrisy

On the left and the right, it is true
We see "leaders" who haven't a clue
Their response to, "But why,
Do the rules you defy?"
 "Do as I say, and not as I do!"

Valor and Discretion

Trump forcefully issued his veto
While gobbling a giant burrito
His party, said "no,"
In a rare, gutsy blow
While trying to vote incognito.

Pardons

The pardons continue to flow

Where they'll stop, we don't really know

No respect for the law

Autocrats watch in awe

Thus ends Trump's reality show.

Resilience

The electors moved forward a nation
Facing threats amidst calls for cessation
But they've now clearly spoken
The States bent, but not broken
Let's give them a standing ovation.

Maritime Transport

Trump pushed Georgia to "find" some more votes
Based on unconfirmed stories he floats
The secretary of state
Would not swallow the bait
So Trump said he'd just bring them in boats.

Citizen Insurrectionists

Determined to "save" the US

From ills only they could redress

They packed Capitol dome

Like the Forum in Rome

The last days of the emperor's excess.

Elected Insurrectionists

There were those in our Congress who tried

To change votes with some deals on the side

It cost them the Senate

Clinging still to their tenet

Even once the mob's siege was denied.

Callousness

With yet millions of people to feed
As finances continue to bleed
Republicans claim
What to them seems fair game
"Give us what we *want* to give them what they *need*."

Deep Thoughts

With a major decision to make
To approve the $2,000 or flake
All eyes turned to old Mitch
Sure to craft a bold pitch
While deep down he thought, "Let them eat cake!"

Amnesia

Since Biden's first term begins soon

The GOP's starting to croon

"It's our job to reverse

The deficit curse"

Forgetting they'd let it balloon.

Startling Discoveries

The scientist Deborah Birx

Discovered a wrench in the works

The Commander-in-Chief

Never once read his brief

Said he, "Clorox might have some real perks!"

Stubborn Facts

America's doctor? That's Fauci

Who always made Trump kinda grouchy

He risked getting the axe

For conveying the facts

Replacing with smarts Trump's debauchery.

The Press

We've watched a decline of the press
Who helped us get into this mess
Still not all news is fake
Unless we should take
Those tweets hammered out in distress.

Real Fake News

Trump's pushing out Fox for Newsmax
Redirecting his endless attacks
Why on earth does he fight?
For right there in plain sight
Clearly neither one cares for the facts.

Cheerleader-in-Chief

Fox has a star anchor named Hannity

Whose central concern is his vanity

Praise Trump all the time

Feed the base a new crime

What could he be missing? Why Sanity!

Sycophants

Trump was worshipped each day by Lou Dobbs

Who had once seemed to care about jobs

In his show filled with praise

He echoed a craze

Most strikingly spelled out by Hobbes.

Perpetual Breaking News

The transition wave spurred CNN

So they ran "Breaking News" without end

With Wolf, King, and dear Cooper

And effects indeed super

For junkies, true election zen.

Another Saturday Night Live (SNL)

There's nothing like Saturday Night
Every week Trump tunes in with a fright
All alone in his room
He'll just watch and he'll fume
"Not funny, but could they be right?"

Detox

Shall we pity the news team at Fox?
Might they launch a campaign of detox?
Always cheering for Trump
'Til he fell in a slump
Would that they could think out of the box.

Pretentiousness

Fox News had a star host named Tucker

Who thought every liberal a sucker

Sporting snappy bow ties

He was sure he looked wise

Though deep down he was just a dumb clucker.

Satire

Fabled humorist Andy Borowitz

Skewered Trump while humming to Horowitz

His humor was biting

His take-downs exciting

As he presaged the best of tomorrow's fits.

Late-Night Comics

Bill, Jimmy, Seth, Trevor and Stephen

Roasted Trump on most nights to get even

They helped us unwind

Which was so very kind

When there wasn't much left to believe in.

IV.
Emboldened Autocrats & Embattled Allies

Farewells

As momentum for Joe Biden swells
World leaders begin their farewells
Some are sad Trump will go
Many others less so
And they all know for whom toll the bells.

Infatuation

Love letters from one Kim Jong-Un
Made Trump unabashedly swoon
And their many close meetings
Filled with warm, manly greetings
Made one heck of a wacky cartoon.

Buyer's Remorse

Putin finally recognized Biden
Who'd been wondering where he'd been hidin'
 "Trump never delivered
Just sat there and quivered
All the more as he saw his loss widen."

Autocrat Nirvana

Two leaders named Orban and Duda
Worshipped Trump as if he were the Buddha
He stayed out of their fights
And ignored human rights
Never taking a stand where he shoulda.

Jewish Worry

Netanyahu now frequently grieves

"There goes Don, we were thicker than thieves

Condoned 'us versus them'

Favored Jerusalem

What oh what will I do when he leaves?"

Conning a Con

Shrewd autocrat Erdogan

Surmised Trump to be ripe for a con

Had him sell out the Kurds

With a few empty words

Knowing well that soon Trump would be gone.

Fallen Idols

Bolsonaro just couldn't believe it

Trump had lost and then couldn't unweave it

Blamed the loss on the 'sissies'

In his own mind 'Ulysses'

Lost his mojo and could not retrieve it.

Fan Clubs

The Indian leader named Modi

Thought Trump to be simply a toady

Houston gave him the chance

To expand their bromance

With Trump star-struck just like a roadie.

Unwelcome News

Trump's defeat reached a sad MBS
Who realized he'd face some duress
 "Trump turned quite the blind eye
We could count on the guy
But with Joe we may be in a mess."

Indifference

Supreme ruler of China was Xi
Who took news of Trump's loss with some glee
Sent his wishes to Joe
But they traveled quite slow
On a boat going up the Yangtze.

Barks & Bites

Mexico's Obrador heard the news
As he'd hoped that old Trump would not lose
"He barked 'bout the wall
But did not bite at all
And Biden knew it was a ruse!"

Juicy Subplots

Trump brought the G7 disorder
In his bid to upend the world order
Her husband diverted
The First Lady flirted
With the leader just north of the border.

Small Pleasures

Canadian leader Trudeau

Rejoiced hearing news Trump would go

"He pushed changing NAFTA

Though we didn't haveta

And he had such a strange orange glow."

Relief

When the news reached Monsieur Macron

He eagerly picked up the phone

"C'est vrai, Biden won?

And Trump is now done?"

"No more handshakes!" he scowled with a groan.

Happy Endings

Upon hearing America's news
As she woke from a relaxing snooze
We're told Merkel cried out
Without the slightest doubt:
"It was not just my dream – he did lose!"

The Ides of November

Boris sent congrats from the UK
It was time Trump got out of the way
Once brothers in arms
He'd tired of his charms
As Trump muttered, "Et tu, Brute?"

Intuition

When informed that Biden had won
Zelensky hummed, "Here comes the sun!"
"Trump insulted Ukraine
The call was insane
I know a joke when I see one!"

Flattery

That bright former premier from Japan
From the start hatched a most cunning plan
 "With Don Trump," Abe said
"We must inflate his head
Call him 'great' just as much as we can."

Schadenfreude

At NATO's Summit, Trump shoved him aside

A display of raw ego and pride

Back in Montenegro

He watched Trump's tales of woe

With a joy he'd not bother to hide.

Positive Energy

Khamenei, Supreme leader of Iran

Was never a Donald Trump fan

When he heard Trump was beaten

His demeanor did sweeten

As he joyfully read the Koran.

Holy Words

From the glorious pen of the Pope
Come wise words meant to give us all hope
"In the new year ahead
We will lessen our dread
As the US gets rid of that dope."

Testing Neutrality

The Swiss like to flaunt their neutrality
They've not criticized Trump's venality
And as he is leaving
They will not be grieving
Unless he seeks Swiss nationality.

Limericks for Post-Election Sanity

Epilogue
Reflection & Appreciation

Democracy

On this hallowed Inaugural Day
There is only one thing left to say
All across our great land
Raise your voice, take a stand
"Our republic's intact — let's keep it that way!"

I want to conclude on a serious note. As this book was going to press, the US Capitol was attacked by a large, angry mob, resulting in casualties, and the former president was impeached for a second time — the first time either has occurred in US history. At the same time, the COVID-19 pandemic has continued to rage across the country, indeed the world, causing unthinkable degrees of pain and suffering, and unspeakable numbers of lost lives. Never did I imagine that in my lifetime I would witness such flagrant erosion of the democratic fabric of the US, coupled with a president's incompetence and indifference to a pandemic and its devastating effects. I am reminded of the prescient words of one of the country's founders, Benjamin Franklin, who cautioned: "A republic, if you can keep it."

Following years of chaos, tumult, and corruption, Trump and his administration have experienced an inglorious collapse, with the president in extreme isolation in his final days, especially as compared to his bluster and ubiquitous news presence prior to the riots. This contrast leads me to recall the words of T.S. Eliot, in "The Hollow Men":

This is the way the world ends
This is the way the world ends
This is the way the world ends
Not with a bang but a whimper.

And yet, while we are witnessing assaults on our ways of life and, indeed, our lives themselves, there are rays of hope, and I do believe strongly in the enduring human spirit and in the resilience of American democracy. I believe wholeheartedly that Joe Biden and his team of 'determined restorers' will make real strides in restoring America's democratic foundations, in rebuilding the country's alliances, and in asserting its intention to return to an important leadership role in the world, once again championing core values of democracy and human rights. This sentiment is driven in large part by the faith I have in the better angels of our nature, despite everything, and in our ability to rise above the darkness and to confront the challenges we face.

And finally, we can take solace in the many brave men and women who have honored and defended the Constitution in standing up to tyranny and making the election and transition to a Biden-Harris administration possible. We owe a great debt to these heroes, including: **patriots**, who have spoken truth to power, especially the courageous **whistleblowers**, who have accepted the risks and consequences in trying to call out abuses throughout the past four years and also during the transition, in particular; **election workers** in polling locations and in vote-counting facilities, working tirelessly through long nights, while being criticized, threatened, and denounced; **judges** across the country, Democrat and Republican, who have defended our laws and Constitution in the face of false allegations of fraud, becoming the precious line of defense that was required, and the **electors,** who did their job in the face of extreme pressure and threats, to cement the fair vote count and to pave the way for the new administration to take on all the many responsibilities with which it will be entrusted. Finally, our gratitude goes to **US voters**, who turned out in the midst of the pandemic and all of the strife and recriminations to vote in historically high numbers and to exercise their right to have a say in who is entrusted with running the country, so that all in our divided nation can have access to life, liberty, and the pursuit of happiness.

Gregg Robins is passionate about democratic values, justice, respect for our fellow human beings, and as much laughter as possible. A native New Yorker, who hails proudly from the Bronx, and now a longtime Swiss resident, Gregg is an author of fiction and non-fiction works. He recently released his first children's book, "Silenzio, Sound the Alarm!" He is also a singer-songwriter, and especially proud of his song "Morning in America," released in 2008 to mark Barack Obama's historic election victory. Founder of Robins Advising, Gregg once dropped out of the Bronx High School of Science before eventually receiving a PhD from Oxford University, where he was a Marshall Scholar. Gregg is the proud father of three millennial daughters — Gabriella, Casey, and Raquel - and he currently lives in Geneva, Switzerland, with his wife Karen.

Charity Russell is a children's book illustrator and writer. Her books include 'Mummy's Got MS', 'Light and The Window Book'. Originally from Zambia, she moved to the U.K. as a teenager and now lives in Bristol, England with her husband, two children and their dog Frank. www.charityrussell.com

Karen Olson-Robins is an activist, community organizer and coach. She has also been engaged in a lifelong struggle to improve the grammar and vocabulary of friends, family and all those who have the temerity to speak English in her presence. She was delighted to play a small part in the creation of this book.